CW00920151

The Observation and Assessment of Children in the Early Years

by
Dr Hannah Mortimer

A QEd Publication

Published in 2001
Reprinted in 2008

© Hannah Mortimer

ISBN 978 1 898873 21 1

British Library Cataloguing
A catalogue record for this book is available from the British Library.

Published by QEd Publications, 39 Weeping Cross, Stafford ST17 0DG
Tel: 01785 620364
Fax: 01785 607797
Web site: www.qed.uk.com
Email: orders@qed.uk.com

Printed by Gutenberg Press, Malta.

Contents

Introduction

Who this book is for

This book will be useful for early years staff working in a variety of early years settings: playgroups, private nurseries, day nurseries and schools. It will also be helpful for individuals training on NVQ or pre-school diploma courses and of interest to childminders, parents and carers of children in their early years.

What is assessment?

If early years assessment is to be worthwhile it should, as Wolfendale (1993) points out, have a clear purpose, be ongoing, include parent(s), and reflect cultural and linguistic background. By the 1980s, the term 'assessment' had come to suggest an objective, mechanical process of measurement. It might have involved a reading test, a 'screening' test for learning difficulties, or an IQ test. In recent years, assessment has moved more into the arena of curriculum; if we wish to 'assess' the point that children have reached in their learning, it makes sense to look at what we are aiming to teach in the first place. So assessment has come to mean an observation of how a child learns and plays now and of what approaches are most helpful to support that learning in the future.

In 1990, the Rumbold Report (DES, 1990) looked at the quality of educational experiences offered to three and four year-olds. It suggested that we should take care not to over-concentrate on formal teaching and on the attainment of a specific set of targets. Instead, it proposed systematic and regular observation-based assessment of children in all areas of their development, and record-keeping based on contributions from the educator, parent and child which would feed into learning and teaching. A balance has to be struck between formal teaching and an ongoing interaction between adult and child designed to encourage them to play, learn, develop and feel good about themselves as learners.

In this context, 'assessment' comes to acquire a wider meaning. It ceases to be a means of measuring something inside the child's head; some elusive 'potential' or 'IQ'. It ceases to become a measure of where the child has reached on a set of curriculum criteria. Instead, it becomes a continuous process of seeing what a child has learned or understood, planning what to teach next, and noting how successfully the child learns. It involves, in other words, both adults interacting and children learning.

How to use this book

In this book, you will find some practical examples of how you can assess and observe children learning and adults interacting. Chapter One introduces the idea of using assessment to establish starting points for teaching and learning, and applies to all children. Chapter Two looks at one area of assessment, that of identifying and assessing children who might have special educational needs (SEN). It suggests doing so within the context of identifying the individual needs of all children, rather than adopting a separate set of procedures.

You will be introduced to the different ways in which you can use observation in Chapter Three. You will also read about a particularly child-centred form of observation and assessment, play-based assessment. Chapter Four describes the assessment which might be carried out by other professionals in your community and how they might work with you.

In Chapter Five, we think about ways of involving children and adults in assessment and planning. There are references and useful resources listed at the end of the book.

Chapter One

Establishing starting points for teaching and learning

The main assessment techniques used in the early years have been described by Hutchin (1999) as talking to parents and carers, talking to the child, making an observation, listening to or participating in a conversation with the child, examining a sample of something the child has done, getting the child to perform a particular task and administering a test.

These assessments are relevant whether we are making an assessment to establish a 'starting point' for our teaching and to monitor progress, or whether we are making an assessment because we feel that a child might have SEN. When you define 'assessment' in this flexible way, you can see that it is impossible to separate your assessment from your ongoing planning, teaching and monitoring. The one is a necessary part of the other, and each feeds into and informs the next, forming a cycle.

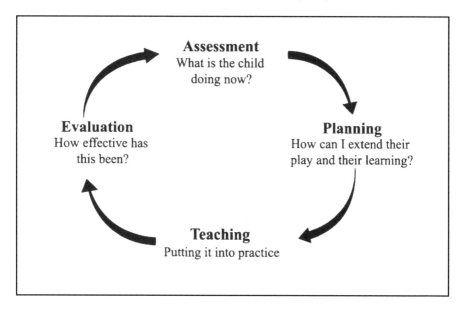

Assessment
What is the child
doing now?

Evaluation
How effective has
this been?

Planning
How can I extend their
play and their learning?

Teaching
Putting it into practice

Linking assessment to curriculum planning

The *Early Years Foundation Stage* (2007) provides a helpful framework for assessing children in the early years. It links children's learning closely with practitioners' teaching and illustrates how the one is inextricably linked with the other. Even when children learn spontaneously, it is through the experiences and opportunities that others, both children and adults, provide. The extension and development of this learning often depends on the sensitivity of the adults in observing how and what the children are learning and how they can use the child's motivation, interest and success to take this further.

In the same way, a child's individual needs might be identified within the six areas of learning through an inclusive process of observing where each child is 'at' in each stage of learning. By providing every opportunity for each child to make progress and by carefully monitoring those whose learning needs do not appear to be met, the practitioner will already have identified those who have special educational needs. For example, there may be children who remain around the very first stage of learning despite the fact that the practitioner has provided the same learning opportunities as for the others.

The questions below could be used as starting points when assessing how children progress within the six areas of learning. They might be used to identify and plan for a child's individual needs and to work out what to teach next. (Author's note: genders have been used randomly to simplify usage.)

Personal, social and emotional development

- Thinking of his self-help skills, have you been able to help him become independent on the toilet yet? Can he take off his anorak now, eat a biscuit, drink from a cup?

- Looking at the relationships she has formed in your setting, is she playing alongside other children now? Is she sharing, watching others, smiling?

- Is his behaviour quiet and withdrawn? Does he respond to 'no'? Can he accept rules with reminders?

Communication, language and literacy
- Can she understand single words and labels? Does she use single words? Can she point, follow simple directions, and listen within a group?

Problem solving, reasoning and numeracy
- Does he understand 'big'/'small'? Can he count to three? Does he understand 'more' and 'all gone'? Will he join in simple number rhymes with actions?

Knowledge and understanding of the world
- Is she aware of her surroundings? Can she follow the familiar routines of the group? Does she ask and answer simple questions?

Physical development
- Thinking of his gross motor skills, is he walking steadily? Can he jump, run, throw with an approximate aim and kick a ball?
- Looking at his fine motor skills, is he scribbling with a pencil? Can he pour water, build blocks and turn pages?

Creative development
- Does she join in during action rhyme sessions? Can she move independently to music? Does she enjoy paints? Will she paste with glue and use collage?

Summary

The following questions might help the early years professional to reflect on the ways in which they are assessing the needs of young children.

Reflecting on assessment

- Does your assessment have a clear purpose?
- Is it an ongoing process?
- How do you include parent(s) and carers?
- Does it reflect cultural and linguistic background?
- Does it show how the child responds to teaching and intervention?
- Does it fit practically within the teaching and planning you do for all the children?

So far we have considered how to assess children's progress in order to plan, deliver and monitor their early years curriculum. In the next chapter, we think about a possible outcome from this assessment – that of identifying a child's special educational needs.

Chapter Two

Identifying and assessing special educational needs

When you are identifying a child's special educational needs for the first time, you are not identifying a label or a condition within a child, but looking at their whole behaviour and learning and how they respond to your particular setting and approaches. If you think about assessment in this way, you will see that you do not have to be an 'expert' in special educational needs; it is your growing expertise in how children learn and develop that is important.

The *SEN Code of Practice* (DfES, 2001) advises settings to adopt approaches for assessing and monitoring children's SEN that:

• identify children's areas of weakness which require extra attention,

• assess children's performance, identifying strengths as well as weaknesses so that the rate of progress resulting from special educational provision can be monitored.

Does an assessment of SEN need to be qualitatively different from the assessments used for all the children? Many would argue that we should be devising inclusive assessment procedures that are as useful in identifying the needs of all children as they are for identifying SEN. The fundamental principles and practices of early years assessment must apply to all children and the best assessment practices used in any early years setting should also improve our ability to identify special educational needs.

Therefore, each setting needs to develop approaches and tools which can be used to identify a child's needs in that setting. If an assessment is to work for the setting and for the child, then it has to be manageable and useful. It also needs to be reliable and valid – in other words, not based on 'assumptions' but on real evidence of what children actually do, able to be observed by all who live, play and learn with the child.

Identifying specific conditions or special educational needs?

In this book, we are discussing the assessment of all children and, now that we are also discussing those with special educational needs, I have chosen to approach these special educational needs from the perspective of all children's individual needs. This is partly because, in a truly inclusive approach, 'child' will come first and 'condition' second. A 'child who has SEN' has a different ring about it to 'an SEN child' (or 'an epileptic' and 'an autistic').

Each child is a unique individual whose needs may not fall neatly into given categories or 'conditions'. This can be heartbreaking for a family struggling to come to terms with their child's special educational needs and desperate for a 'label' to provide some sort of 'handle' on the situation. Nevertheless, it is a fact that the vast majority of special educational needs in the early years will have no set 'cause' or 'label'. There is sometimes a concern that, without the 'label', an early years practitioner cannot set out to understand the condition and therefore meet the needs. And because they are not 'experts' in identifying the label, they cannot make steps towards meeting the needs.

However, it is knowledge of the needs that leads to action. It becomes more pragmatic and constructive to speak of 'needs' than of 'conditions'. Suddenly this allows the early years practitioner a way forward. They are already experienced in how children learn in the early stages of development and the *Early Years Foundation Stage* (2007) can provide a framework both for providing the early years curriculum and identifying needs and planning action within it. We will look at how this might be done on page 18.

What is meant by 'disability'?

The Disability Discrimination Act, 1995 defines disability as a physical or mental impairment which has a substantial and long-term adverse effect on a person's ability to carry out normal day-to-day activities. Physical or mental disability includes sensory impairments such as hearing or visual impairments. Hidden disabilities are also covered (for example mental illness and mental health problems, learning difficulties, dyslexia and conditions such as diabetes and epilepsy). People with severe disfigurements are also covered.

The SEN and Disability Act, 2001 draws on the Disability Discrimination Act, 1995 and clearly sets out requirements on those providing school education. It is, therefore, very important that awareness of the issues surrounding disability and special educational needs are raised and training increased amongst educators. The SEN framework makes an increasing assumption that children with special educational needs will be educated in mainstream settings. The SEN and Disability Act *strengthens* the general *duty* to provide a mainstream school place for a child with special educational needs.

The definition of SEN is widely understood as being about children and young people with learning difficulties. It is important to recognise that the definition of children with learning difficulties *includes* children with a disability where any special educational provision needs to be made. This does not mean that children with a disability necessarily have learning difficulties, or that only disabled children with learning difficulties have special educational needs. It does mean that children with a disability have special educational needs *if they have any difficulty in accessing education* and if they need any special educational provision to be made for them.

When do we decide that a child might have SEN?

In any early years setting, there are likely to be children with many different ages and at very different stages of development. Each child is a unique individual who brings his or her own experiences and particular pattern of developing and behaving. In time, it might become clear to those working with a child that there are special educational needs. How does the practitioner know when to be concerned if a child seems to be developing differently? What is the legal definition of a 'special educational need'?

Definition of Special Educational Needs

A child has special educational needs if he or she has a *learning difficulty* which calls for *special educational provision* to be made for him or her.

A child has a *learning difficulty* if he or she:

(a) has a significantly greater difficulty in learning than the majority of children of the same age; or

(b) has a disability which prevents or hinders them from making use of educational facilities of a kind generally provided for children of the same age in schools within the area of the local education authority;

(c) is under five and falls within the definition at (a) or (b) above or would do if special educational provision was not made for the child.

A child must not be regarded as having a learning difficulty solely because the language or medium of communication of the home is different from the language in which he or she is or will be taught.

Special educational provision means:

(a) for a child over two, educational provision which is additional to, or otherwise different from, the educational provision made generally for children of the child's age in maintained schools, other than special schools, in the area;

(b) for a child under two, educational provision of any kind.

(from Education Act 1996, Section 312)

The Education Act (1996) sets out that any difficulty must be *significant*, over and above what you would expect from the child's age, and affect the child's ability to access the play and learning activities that your setting provides. It is not sufficient for the child to be *different*. So to speak a language different from the majority of the group, or to suffer a medical condition that does not affect day-to-day learning, will not represent a 'special educational need'.

Children might be described as having SEN for many different reasons; perhaps they have a physical disability, perhaps their development is delayed, perhaps they have a language and communication difficulty, or there are behaviour or emotional difficulties. Early years practitioners now have a duty to recognise and identify any special educational needs within their setting so that they can plan what action they can take to support and help the child.

The *SEN Code of Practice* (DfES, 2001) suggests that the triggers for intervention through 'Early Years Action Plus' could be a practitioner's concern about a child who, despite receiving appropriate early education experiences:

- makes little or no progress even when teaching approaches are particularly targeted to improve the child's identified area of weakness;

- continues working at levels significantly below those expected for children of a similar age in certain areas;

- presents persistent emotional and/or behavioural difficulties, which are not ameliorated by the behaviour management techniques usually employed in the setting;

- has sensory or physical problems, and continues to make little or no progress despite the provision of personal aids and equipment;

- has communication and/or interaction difficulties, and requires specific individual interventions in order to access learning.

(Note: *The SEN Code of Practice* (DfES, 2001) referred to applies in England. N.Ireland, Scotland and Wales use different terminology.)

Early warning signs

Most settings would allow a child to settle into their group and to benefit from their structure and opportunities for at least a term before assuming that the child's needs might be 'special'. Settings are also encouraged to have a flexible enough curriculum with an individual enough approach which allows them to move seamlessly into approaches that are going to foster and encourage the child's learning and development from their first days in the setting.

The purpose of asking 'what helps?' along with 'are there any difficulties?' provides you with information about whether you need to make plans which go beyond the individual approaches you would normally take for the range of individuals in your care. If you find that you need to target and monitor a child particularly closely in order for them to gain access to the early years curriculum, then this is tantamount, in the current terminology, to saying that the child has 'special educational needs'. The 'label' or 'condition' cannot be separated from what it is the practitioner needs to do about it; it is both together that provide you with information about whether or not a child has special educational needs.

When identifying special educational needs for the first time, the following range of questions to early years educators and to parents might be helpful in establishing whether the child might have special educational needs.

Speech and language

Can the child's spoken language only be understood by familiar adults in a familiar context? Is he mostly silent? Does he have difficulty in following a simple instruction in a familiar context? Does he find difficulty in socially interacting, even with an interested adult? Does he use only single words or learned phrases to express himself? Does he hardly ever respond to adult suggestion when playing? How does he make his needs known? What can adults do to help him understand more clearly? Does he receive help for a speech, language or communication difficulty? What approaches have helped?

Behaviour

Is the child's behaviour extremely challenging both at home and in your setting? Once settled in, does she show no signs of responding to your group's routines and rules; is this similar at home? Does she seem to be very unhappy, quiet and withdrawn, even once she has had a chance to settle in with familiar adults and familiar children? Are parents concerned about her 'clinginess' or withdrawal at home? What seems to help? Have there been major events in her life that she has had to cope with? Will she make a close attachment to a familiar adult in the setting?

Cognitive development

Is the child at least a year behind what you would expect for his age? Is this despite his having had all the usual experiences to learn and to play and despite your providing opportunities for learning and play familiar to his cultural context? You might like to use a developmental checklist as a guide, making sure that it is appropriate to his cultural and linguistic background. What are his learning styles? What helps to maintain his concentration? What things motivate and stimulate him?

Physical development

Does the child have a physical difficulty or disability that prevents his joining in the activities with the other children? How does this affect him? What resources, aids or methods of support help? Can he dress/feed himself/go to the toilet (etc.) unassisted? Where is he most vulnerable? What helps?

Hearing

Has the child had recurrent ear infections or colds with fluctuating hearing? Has he failed two successive hearing tests? Has he seen a hearing specialist or had grommets inserted? Have parents ever been worried that he is not hearing them? Does he have aids and how do these help? Do adults need to communicate with him in a particular way? How does he make his own needs known?

Vision

Can the child see clearly, as far as you know? Have parents ever been concerned about her vision? Perhaps the setting feels that she is not seeing clearly, or not making sense of what is seen; have parents seen this kind of response at home? How does she compensate for any difficulty? What approaches seem to help?

Using Welcome Profiles

All these questions are starting points in the common sense approach that can be applied to finding out more about individual children's needs and how to meet them. You might like to design and use a 'Welcome Profile' as a helpful tool when gathering information about a child entering a new setting. Put together a simple checklist which you can ask new parents and carers to complete, or ask the questions as part of an admission interview. You may also find the *ALL ABOUT ME* materials helpful (Wolfendale, 1998).

Think through your setting's regular day and ask for practical information in order to work out where and when a child might need additional help or support. Are there any medical problems you need to know about? Is the child on any regular medication? Are there other professionals who help the child? Are there any problems with hearing and seeing? How does the child make his/her needs known? What things make the child really happy? Is anything worrying the parents/carers or the child about starting with you? Is there anything else they would like to tell you about the child?

Using the early years curriculum

Here is one example of how the *Early Years Foundation Stage* framework (2007) might be used to identify special educational needs. Practitioners might like to develop similar examples based on their particular settings and the range of needs they meet there.

Identifying SEN: Physical development

Does a four year-old child show little interest in physical play? Is this despite the fact that the adult has:

- provided safe spaces for the child to move in?
- talked to the child and helped them find new ways to move and to explore their surroundings?
- offered a range of stimuli to generate movement including music, songs, action rhymes and stories?
- provided a variety of indoor and outdoor activities over several weeks?

Does the child have difficulty in walking, running, climbing and jumping? Is this despite the fact that the adult has:

- provided safe props and equipment to encourage movement and balance?
- planned opportunities for children to tackle a range of surfaces and levels?
- provided opportunities for children to repeat and change their actions so that they can think about, refine and improve them?

Does the child have difficulty in manipulating objects and materials? Is this despite the adult:

- providing objects that can be safely handled?
- encouraging the child to sit or stand in the correct position?
- giving the individual child opportunities to develop fine motor skills by teaching and encouraging them?

Chapter Three

Methods of observation

In Chapter 1, we concluded that we gain information about children all the time we are with them. The observations we make affect what we provide for them. What are the different methods we can use for observing children?

Different methods of observation

We might carry out a **fly on the wall observation**, observing a child over a period of time (say 30 minutes) and writing down what they are doing and how they are interacting in clear, unambiguous terms. We might also use a **timed observation** by noting what a child is doing, say, every five minutes regardless of what is happening in the nursery or group. We might involve the child in an activity and make a **participant observation** of what the child does and how they interact and learn with us. **On the spot observations** involve the adult noting down significant events or achievements after they happen in a kind of running diary.

If we are providing an assessment as part of a 'statutory assessment of SEN', perhaps because a child's SEN are significant enough to mean that a 'Statement of SEN' might be necessary, then the observations we make have to be reliable for our planning and provision to be appropriate. More formal or structured methods of observation (which have been developed to be reliable and valid across observers and situations) are sometimes used in these situations.

This is why some settings use *standardized checklists* of observation to help their assessments and planning. A standardized checklist tells you what particular skills or behaviours are typical of a certain age or stage. Some settings feel that this helps them to know what is 'normal' and when to be concerned. Other settings prefer to look at their curriculum, set out to teach to any weaknesses, and to become concerned when progress is not forthcoming despite planned support and teaching.

Observational methods used may vary according to the information sought. **Selective observation**, for example, focuses on specific areas of the child's behaviour chosen by an adult. Here are some examples.

1. **Behavioural observation** using an **ABC chart** can help to identify any factors that may be affecting the child's behaviour. By recording the 'Antecedent' (what happened before the behaviour took place), the 'Behaviour' (exactly what the child did) and the 'Consequence' (what happened as a result of the behaviour), a clearer view of the context of the behaviour can be gained.

What led up to it?	Behaviour	What happened next?
Beth was playing with the farm animals and Tara asked for one.	Beth hit Tara on the chest.	Tara cried and Beth tipped all the animals onto the floor. Mrs Grainger comforted Tara and helped Beth say 'sorry' and pick up the animals.

2. **Spider's web observation** can look at the child's ability to sustain in-depth play experiences while being supported by an adult. Activities provided are listed around the edge of a circle (the adult support is included as an activity), the observer can chart the movement of the child in the group. The time spent at each activity can be noted at the perimeters of the circle. This type of observation can also highlight a child's particular interests or areas that are avoided.

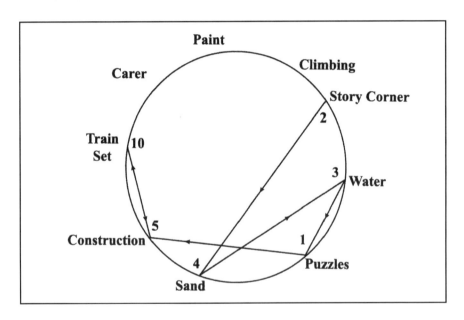

3. **Tracking observations** can be useful in observing an unsupported child around the setting. They indicate the areas of play experience that may be targeted for the child. A rough plan of the layout is drawn and the movement of the child is recorded by arrowed lines, with numbers to indicate the length of time spent at each activity.

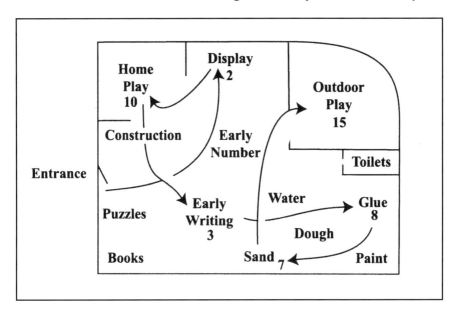

These detailed observations can provide a lot of information with regard to the child's level of skill, what the child gains from the activity, the social context and level of interaction, and the child's use of language. Any observation should run alongside the ongoing planning and assessment that will be done for all the children wherever possible.

Checklists

Some checklists are highly detailed and become useful for a child with significant special educational needs who requires highly detailed planning and help, perhaps through a special support assistant. The 'Portage' checklist (NFER-Nelson, 1987) is one example. Portage is a home teaching scheme for pre-school children with special educational needs and their families. Home visitors help parents complete a detailed assessment of their child's developmental progress using the Portage checklist, set long-term goals for teaching 'next steps' and break these down into manageable weekly tasks for the children to learn. It would not be practicable or necessary to use a detailed checklist such as this for all the children.

A checklist should only be used as a 'coat hanger' on which to hang the careful planning and teaching you will be doing across all areas. It does help the setting and the parents to keep a long-term goal for their child's development, and to highlight areas of strength and weakness that need working on.

The *Playladders* checklist

The *Playladders* (Mortimer, 2000b) checklist can be used with all children in the *Early Years Foundation Stage* and fits in well with everyday activities. It was devised as a developmental checklist based not on specific areas of development, but on early years activities themselves. This kind of approach has been adapted in the *Trackers 0-5* observation records (published by QEd Publications) which look at how children typically progress through these age bands. These kinds of records should always be used as a framework for assessing and tracking progress rather than a curriculum in themselves.

Early years staff are encouraged to play alongside the child as part of their regular activities within a group of children. By observing how the child is playing, it becomes easy to visualize and record the stage on the Playladder later, once the children have left. Play thus proceeds uninterrupted by the assessment and recording. Once the play behaviour is recorded on the checklist, a 'next step on the ladder' is suggested, and this new skill can be encouraged or taught at a future play session. This is helpful towards providing activities at a level appropriate to the child, or adapting an existing activity so that the child is always included.

Other recording methods

In their book *Making Assessment Work*, Drummond, Rouse and Pugh (1992) list various approaches to writing down the assessment record and encourage educators to develop their own approach which suits their setting, their curriculum and the particular children. One way is to use a checklist of behaviours or play activities (as in the Portage and Playladders approaches above). Another is to assess under topics using flow-charts and curriculum content (e.g. 'learning about travel', 'learning about water'). 'Schemas of learning' can be used to record children's prevailing patterns of thinking or 'schemas' and yet other approaches might look at the processes through which children learn (such as collaborating, exploring, talking and sharing). The High/Scope Child Anecdotal Record is a method of gathering anecdotal evidence for each child in the nursery under their key experiences in social relations and initiative, music and movement, and cognitive development (creative representation, language and literacy, classification, seriation, number, space and time).

Yet other settings have developed checklists, record sheets or profiles based on the early years curriculum, usually relating to the six areas of learning as set out in the EYFS: communication, language and literacy; knowledge and understanding of the world; personal, social and emotional development; creative development; problem solving, reasoning and numeracy; and physical development.

Play-based assessment

Why does play offer such a useful medium for assessing children's progress and needs? It is a natural means of expression for most children and is something that almost every child can engage in at their own level. It therefore provides a relaxed and positive situation in which children can show of their best and not be subject to 'failure' if they do not respond to the standardized wording or procedures of a psychometric test. Play is the activity within which young children explore and develop new concepts and it can therefore provide a window of how a child is doing so. We are also in a good position to actually intervene and promote that learning; when assessment and intervention are combined in this way, we speak of a 'dynamic assessment'.

Play-based assessment can provide adults with rich information about how children play, learn and respond to adult intervention. Observation studies involving recording how children typically play have been invaluable here and have led to useful observation schedules. Readers might be interested in the *Play-Based Assessment* devised by Sayeed and Guerin (2000). Play-based assessments lent themselves to the development of more dynamic forms of assessment which involve looking at how children respond to teaching.

Dynamic assessment

We have spoken of some of the dilemmas and doubts arising from using static psychometric assessments. Some practitioners are now looking towards more ongoing and dynamic methods of assessing children's learning. Dynamic approaches to assessment involve the assessor actually working with the child to encourage active participation in the learner. The focus is on the process of learning and how a child arrived at a solution. An effort is made to modify the way a child approaches learning so that they can be helped to become a more effective learner.

The interactions between assessor and child which assist the child's cognitive development are known as 'mediation' and the aim is to understand through intervention what best supports the child's learning. Many people see this as a better measure of 'potential' than a psychometric score or IQ. One example of a dynamic assessment approach used in early years is the 'bunny bag' of toys used in the Let's Play approach in Newcastle-upon-Tyne (Waters, 1999). Toys were selected on the basis of how attractive they were to the children, how flexible they were in allowing the children to demonstrate a range of play and learning, and how practicable they were to purchase and carry around. The assessor is encouraged to mediate the child's play by helping them feel at ease, focusing their attention, helping them to generalize, helping them to plan, helping them break a task down and helping them feel successful.

A practical guide in the *Let's Play* pack gives examples of how this might be done during an assessment. The assessment guide lists typical repertoires of play and learning for each toy used in the assessment, and there are very approximate age norms for each. A second guide lists how children approach play and learning, what the assessor did to affect or improve the performance and what the outcome was in the child's response. The assessment therefore measures not only how the child plays with each toy but also how adult support can be used to improve this.

Psychometric testing

If you are concerned that a child might have special educational needs, you may well find that specialist 'testing' has a relevant role to play as a part of the assessment. However, it is early years staff themselves who have the key role in identifying if a child is learning or behaving in a way that requires special educational provision to be made. With the implementation of the *SEN Code of Practice* (DfES, 2001), assessing SEN becomes part of a team effort and cannot be delegated to 'the specialists out there'.

Thus a child may well be 'tested' to establish if their hearing or vision is satisfactory. A speech and language therapist may be involved in establishing whether children can understand abstract vocabulary and how they are expressing themselves and communicating. In doing so, he or she will be using many of the methods of assessment we have listed (talking to parents and carers, talking to the child, making observations, listening to or participating in a conversation with a child, examining samples of the child's language, getting a child to perform a particular task) but this may be done in a 'standardized' way. Because the 'test' has been delivered using a standard approach that has been applied to very many children, the therapists will be able to state with confidence that 'most children at a stage of, say, two years tend to understand language at this level'. This kind of test is described as 'psychometric' since the scores can be linked statistically (at a given level of statistical 'confidence') to a large sample of children so that the tester can state the 'norm' for any age.

Another example of a psychometric test is the IQ test that originated at the beginning of the last century and played a large role in educational assessment and selection. The scores on the assessment are distributed in a 'normal distribution' (or bell-shaped curve when you plot score against numbers of children scoring at that level). The 'average' score for any age will be 100, with only around 2% of the population scoring below 70 or above 130. So 'absolute' was the interpretation of these scores that educationalists would speak of 'education subnormality' in terms of children scoring an IQ lower than 70 on a single intellectual assessment. Traditionally, the Stanford Binet Tests, followed by the Wechsler Intelligence Scales and later the British Ability Scales, were used regularly to diagnose and to make predictions about 'potential'.

There has been a growing discomfort among many psychologists about using these tests, or at least about using them in an isolated way. Critics of intelligence tests typically state that IQ tests label children inappropriately, do not offer information about curriculum planning, are culturally biased and are not as statistically reliable or valid as their developers claim. Educators and parents sometimes saw a child's IQ score as a fixed and unchangeable measure that was part of a child's internal make-up, rather than a measure of performance on a certain test on a certain day.

Nevertheless, IQ tests are still widely used as measures of a child's 'ability'. This rather assumes that 'ability' is fixed and stable over time and therefore determines the child's future learning. If we believe this, we need to be wary. We may in reality be discriminating against the child by having expectations that are fixed and that limit the child's opportunities to learn and to develop.

To counter some of the criticisms levelled against intelligence tests, methods of curriculum-based assessment, criterion-referenced tests and checklists of achievement have been developed. These approaches are usually derived from a series of learning objectives and aim to find out what the child already knows and what might be taught next. By breaking the 'next step' down (using the method of 'task analysis'), each step can be made achievable and successful for the child.

Chapter Four

Assessment by other professionals

Multidisciplinary community teams

Early years professionals have been encouraged to work more closely together for many years now. In the 1980s, there was a rapid growth of Child Development Centres. Children and families were offered diagnosis and multidisciplinary assessment of congenital and acquired handicapping conditions, with treatment and intervention. Medical treatment was available, and advice and provision on aids, adaptations and resources. Advice, counselling and support were generally available to parents and families, and information was available on statutory and voluntary services. The Centres were also able to contribute towards advice on the children's special educational needs.

Since then, there has been a move towards supporting children and their families in their own homes and communities wherever possible, though the Child Development Centres have remained as 'gateways' into services and bases for professional teams and for multidisciplinary assessment. Who are the professionals who work at these Centres or in the community, and what might their roles be in the assessment of any child with whom you might be involved?

Early years support teachers

Support and advisory teachers play a central role at the time of transfer into school, nursery or pre-school. Sometimes they are based at your local education offices (perhaps as part of the Early Years Service or the SEN Support Service) and sometimes they work as part of a multidisciplinary Child Development Team or a community-based Early Years Partnership.

They have particular knowledge of the statutory assessment procedures, and are therefore able to talk families through the process, liaise with schools and education authorities, and set up any introductory visits. Because of their experience and knowledge of how children learn in a range of settings, they are well placed to complete the educational advice in any statutory assessment of a young child's special educational needs. Once a child is placed in a pre-school setting, their parent liaison role usually continues, particularly if problems arise, or where nurseries need advice in setting individual teaching programmes.

The paediatrician and community doctor

The paediatrician is a specialist children's doctor and offers paediatric and neurological examination. With these investigations and information gained from parents the paediatrician will attempt to identify the cause of problems and provide diagnosis. Early diagnosis, counselling and support usually follow, perhaps with a referral to the local Child Development Centre or Children's Service. Paediatricians also have a role in providing or arranging genetic counselling and in arranging for children to go into hospital where necessary.

Paediatricians also provide the service of monitoring medical condition and needs as the child grows older, and monitoring hearing and vision are an important part of this. Community doctors can also help to liaise with schools and education, and contribute to the statutory assessment of SEN.

The speech and language therapist

Speech and language therapists offer assessment, treatment, advice and counselling to people of all ages with a speech, language or communication disorder and related eating and swallowing problems. They also offer support and advice to carers such as parents, partners and nursing staff to help them understand the nature of the problem and how they can help.

Most speech and language therapists working in multidisciplinary assessment teams are involved in the assessment and treatment of speech, language and communication disorders, including all the skills needed before language and communication can begin to develop. Advice is given on feeding, sucking, mouth and tongue movements, and textures of foods.

Sometimes, advice on alternative and augmentative communication becomes necessary and training is given to other professionals, parents and carers on the use of communication aids and signing systems.

The physiotherapist

Physiotherapists can elect to specialise in children's work. Their aim is to work towards helping the child reach his or her maximum potential. Following assessment and therapeutic diagnosis, the physiotherapist will work closely with parents or carers to establish appropriate goals for the child. This individually planned programme of physiotherapy might cover careful positioning and movement, advice and support, special handling skills, exercise regimes, walking practice, balance and co-ordination exercises, stretching of muscles, chest physiotherapy and special equipment.

Most paediatric physiotherapists are involved in the assessment of gross motor skills and treatment of motor delay. They work particularly with children with physical disabilities and delay, providing advice on handling and care, lifting, positioning, nasal suctioning, inhibiting abnormal reflexes and advising on splints, boots, braces, wheelchairs and buggies, sometimes with overlap with the occupational therapist.

The occupational therapist

Occupational therapists work with children of varying ages whose development is interrupted by physical, psychological, or social impairment or disability. They aim to develop the child's maximum level of independence thereby improving practical life skills which hopefully promotes a better quality of life. Work is carried out in conjunction with the child's family or carer in a variety of settings. They assess gross and fine motor skills, any dyspraxic difficulties, writing, independence skills, visual perception and body awareness, and the need for specialised equipment for home and pre-school including seating, wheelchairs, toilet and bathing aids, adaptive equipment to improve everyday skills. Sometimes they provide a specialist assessment of switches and information technology.

The clinical psychologist

Clinical psychologists are employed by the NHS whereas educational psychologists are usually employed by the Local Education Authority. Some multidisciplinary assessment teams have considerable overlap between educational and clinical psychologist with caseload determined by age and stage, or even geographically. In other teams, these respective roles are determined by the availability of the particular psychologist. Clinical psychologists can offer, in particular, family support and counselling, family therapy, advice and intervention on attachment difficulties, cognitive and developmental assessment, advice on behaviour management, and specialist knowledge of certain conditions, such as autism.

The educational psychologist

Educational psychologists attempt to assist others to find solutions to difficulties, problems or needs to see if, by working together, they can make a difference to the child. They help by clarifying and defining the problem, generating teaching and management approaches, and evaluating the success of these. They tend to work in schools and early years settings alongside teachers and early years educators. They assess learning difficulties and draw up advice.

They can provide specialist assessment of cognitive or learning difficulties, provide assessment and advice based on paradigms of child development and learning theory and the use and interpretation of normative psychometric assessment. Advice on behaviour management is often given. They are able to help colleagues and parents to focus their observations, and also to make useful interpretations of how the child was playing. Sometimes, specialist skills in bereavement counselling, or conflict resolution are called upon.

The social worker

Counselling and family support are offered, usually with the ability to visit the home and assess or support the family situation and dynamics. They have access to social services provision, including day nurseries, respite care, shared caring and pre-school support schemes. Child protection procedures are also a crucial and specific role, with the possible conflict that this can raise for some families.

Chapter Five

Involving children and adults in assessment and planning

Making it meaningful

Try to involve the children themselves in your assessment so that they have a say in what successes you are celebrating and what areas they feel they need help in. What should our overriding principles be when we work with young children to assess and support their individual needs? (Drummond, Rouse and Pugh, 1992.)

- Respect each child for their culture, their ethnicity, their language, their religion, their age and their gender. The methods we choose for assessment and intervention must be appropriate for the child. There must be no danger of bias.

- The care and education of young children are not two separate, discrete activities. In the work we do, quality care is educational and quality education is caring. Therefore, when we work with young children, we need to attend to their whole development and lives and not to certain aspects of it.

- Early years educators inevitably have 'power' when working with children and their families; this needs to be acknowledged and used lovingly, wisely and well.

- Always keep the interests of the child paramount. Assessment and intervention must enhance their lives, their learning and their development. It must 'work' for the child.

You might decide that one of your methods of assessing the children's progress is going to be through a special 'treasure box' for each child in the setting. Ask the children which pieces of work they would like you to photograph, or which pictures should be placed in their special box 'to keep forever'. Spend time helping each child look through their 'treasures' and talk about what they enjoyed and what they would like to do in the future.

As well as involving children in the process of assessment, we should make our very assessment tools as involving, pleasurable and positive for the child as possible. There are ways in which we can ensure the assessment arises naturally from a familiar situation in which the child is enabled to show of his best as well as of his level of need. The *Playladders* checklist and *Music Makers: Music circle times to include everyone* (Mortimer, 2006) provide examples of this kind of assessment.

We are encouraged in the *SEN Code of Practice* (DfES, 2001) to involve children directly in their own assessments and education planning. How can we do this with very young children at the earliest stages of their educational careers? In many senses, early years carers have been exploring ways of making all their assessments meaningful and child-centred for a long time. We look for ways of 'starting where the child is at', 'going with the child', developing home-based services, and sharpening our skills in using play and observation as an assessment tool.

One example of how to involve young children in their own assessments is by using a 'talk-through approach'. This can be used to lead children through their own statutory assessments of special educational needs or their coming change of school; why it is all happening; who they will meet; what will happen next; what they enjoy or wish for in a receiving school; what words they use to describe their special educational needs; and what the actual implications of these needs are for the child.

Taking Part (Mortimer, 2000a) will be helpful here. It provides a practical format for a parent or carer to lead a young child through the process of a statutory SEN assessment, thinking through the answers to certain questions all of which are related to concrete experiences in the child. A shared language is developed for describing the special educational needs concerned and, through this, the child becomes an active participant in the agenda of the assessment. The approach can be followed with only minor adaptations for a 'verbal' child, amending wording and example according to the particular child, culture and situation. For a 'pre-verbal child' or a child who cannot communicate using language, the approach can be used to suggest ways in which a parent or carer can think through the assessment from the child's point of view, thereby serving as an advocate for their view, ensuring that any recommendations also fit the child's own agenda. The end product is a completed questionnaire which can be used to form a child's contribution to the evidence of the statutory assessment.

Using a combination of these play-based approaches, it should become possible to provide not only a child-centred assessment, but a child-involving one also. You have allowed them the right to be heard, gathered from them the essential and relevant information that they are in a position to share with you, and empowered them in the process of the assessment.

Circle time approaches

Using circle time is a useful way to make sure that each child feels included and valued. It allows you to make eye contact with each child individually and to use your attention and encouragement to make all the children feel motivated. You can also use it to assess and address social skills, feelings and friendship. You might find *Learning through Play: Circle Time* (Mortimer, 1998) helpful as it suggests activities for enjoying circle time across the six areas of learning with opportunities for observing and assessment. *Music Makers: Music circle times to include everyone* (Mortimer, 2006) is a method of using a regular music circle time in early years to help all the children look, listen and join in, but also to individually assess and target any child who has SEN.

Working with parents to assess and plan

The involvement of parents is a basic principle of the *SEN Code of Practice* (DfES, 2001). Schools are now required to draw up 'Home-school Agreements' which explain what the school's aims and values are, what its duties towards the pupils are, the responsibilities of parents and what the school expects of its pupils.

What approaches seem to be effective for developing a real partnership between parents and early years practitioners?

- You need to acknowledge the fundamental role that parents have already played in their child's education. So when you speak of assessment, avoid the suggestion that when a child enters your setting their learning is at a 'baseline'. Instead, acknowledge all the play and learning that has already gone on at home.

- Look for ways of sharing the responsibility for learning between home and setting. This is done through mutual respect, ongoing communication and regular information about your aims, assessments and plans.

- Make sure that parents feel welcome in your setting and that there are opportunities for working together with parents, staff and children to assess, teach and learn together.

- Parents need information at all stages of their children's learning and progress (and not just when there is a 'problem').

- Admission procedures should be flexible to allow time for discussion with parents and for children to feel secure in a new setting.

Sharing information on SEN

When a child first starts in a new setting, it is a sensitive time for all parents. Add to this the particular concerns and mixed emotions that parents of a child with SEN might have, and you can understand that sensitive handling will be vital for effective partnership with parents. Will the group cope with my child's needs? Will I as a parent cope with standing back now my child is in nursery?

Invest time before a child joins your setting gathering information and establishing a relationship with child and parents. A home visit is usually helpful, sharing photographs of your group and talking about your typical sessions. Asking positive, open-ended questions can provide information about the child's strengths and about the kind of help that they need. Parents soon feel discouraged if they find themselves listing all the things their child cannot do.

Take time to ask parents what they would like the setting to do to help, taking care they are not left feeling that they have failed in some way. Taking trouble to share the 'good news' from the start, helps any 'bad news' to fall more into context. Above all, settings can show that they care and are trying to work alongside parents to help the child.

Parent checklists

Some checklists and schedules are designed solely for use by the family but the information they provide has proved useful in designing the individual teaching approach for the child. The *ALL ABOUT ME* materials by Sheila Wolfendale (1998) were the first parent checklist to become widely used.

The *ALL ABOUT ME* materials became influential in providing a practical framework for parents and professionals to involve children in their own assessments and planning. They started as a checklist that enabled parents to note down and record from time to time their child's development and progress. The record belonged to the parents and served as a useful basis for discussing ongoing progress with a teacher, playgroup leader or support professional. First it was trialled with over 130 children aged two to six-and-a-half from all over the country, and then revised on the basis of this feedback. It was notable at the time as being written in the first person, from the point of view of the child. The revised edition keeps the contents as before, but the 'Notes for Parents, Carers and their Children' have been revised, and there is a short new section entitled 'Guidance Notes for Early Years Workers in Using *ALL ABOUT ME*'. There are also new illustrations.

ALL ABOUT ME covers seven areas of the child's life and experience: language; playing and learning; doing things for myself; my physical development; my health and my habits; other people and how I behave; my moods and feelings. Though it started as a parent record, it was adopted by many schools and early years settings as part of the personal records and child profiling. It was also taken on board by many LEA Parent Partnership Officers as a way of involving parents and children in the statutory assessment procedures, and an aide-memoire to gathering information from parents.

Involving parents in assessment

Here are some practical ways of involving parents in assessing their child's needs and progress.

- Make a personal invitation to parents to visit you regularly so that you and their child can show off their progress. Use this as a time for finding out what new things the child has learned to do at home as well.

- For various reasons, parents do not always call in to the setting on a daily basis. It is often helpful to invite parents into the setting to share information about their child's achievements, in an informal way, or to arrange a home visit if possible.

- Draw the parents' attention to a specific display, where examples of their child's work can be seen.

- If there have been behaviour problems, show parents what their child has already achieved and progress made within the setting. At the same time, do not make them feel too despondent if there has not been progress at home. Use the 'good news' as a hope for positive changes to come.

- Ask the child to show his parents what he can do, what he can say or what he has learnt.

- Ask parents for their opinions, by allowing opportunities for them to contribute information and share experiences. It is often helpful to set a regular time aside when other demands will not intrude.

- Thank parents regularly for their support.

- Celebrate success with parents. This will ensure an ongoing positive partnership.

- Use a home/pre-school diary to keep in touch regarding their child's progress.

A two-way system of sharing information about a child's success, experiences and opportunities can help in supporting the child.

Assessing progress in your setting

Now that you have read this book, here are some points for you to think about with your colleagues.

- Have you discussed what you think 'assessment' is? What are you assessing and why? Will it make a positive difference to the child?

- Are you familiar with your national framework and *Code of Practice for identifying and assessing SEN*?

- Have you procedures and action plans in place to both identify and assess a child's individual needs in your setting?

- Have you thought carefully about how to share assessment with parents?

- Have you considered ways in which you can establish the child's own views and feelings about the education they are receiving?

- Are you aware of what your support services are and how to access them if you need to?

- Have you thought about how to dovetail your SEN procedures with your approaches for monitoring all the children's needs and progress in your setting?

References

Children Act (1989) London: HMSO.

DES (1990) *Starting with Quality* (The Rumbold Report). London: HMSO.

DfES (2007) *The Early Years Foundation Stage.* Nottingham: DfES Publications.

DfES (2001) *The Special Educational Needs Code of Practice.* Nottingham: DfES Publications.

Disability Discrimination Act (1995) London: HMSO.

Drummond, M. J., Rouse, D. and Pugh, G. (1992) *Making Assessment Work: Values and Principles in Assessing Young Children's Learning.* London: National Children's Bureau and Nottingham: NES Arnold.

Gallow, C. (2007) *Trackers 0-5: Tracking children's progress through the Early Years Foundation Stage.* Stafford: QEd Publications.

Henderson, A. (1994) *Observation and Record Keeping.* London: Pre-school Learning Alliance.

Hutchin, V. (1999) *Right from the Start: Effective Planning and Assessment in the Early Years.* London: Hodder and Stoughton.

Mortimer, H. (1998) *Learning through Play: Circle Time.* Leamington Spa: Scholastic Ltd.

Mortimer, H. (2000a) *Taking Part.* Stafford: QEd Publications.

Mortimer, H. (2000b) *Playladders.* Stafford: QEd Publications.

Mortimer, H. (2006) *Music Makers: Music circle times to include everyone*. Stafford: QEd Publications.

Mortimer, H. (2001) *Special Needs and Early Years Provision*. London: Continuum.

Sayeed, Z. and Guerin, E. (2000) *Early Years Play: A Happy Medium for Assessment and Intervention*. London: David Fulton Publishers.

Special Educational Needs and Disability Act (2001) London: HMSO.

Waters, J. (1999) *Let's Play: A Guide to Interactive Assessment with Young Children*. Newcastle upon Tyne: Educational Psychology Service.

Wolfendale, S. (Ed) (1993) *Assessing Special Educational Needs*. London: Cassell.

Wolfendale, S. (1998, 2nd edition) *ALL ABOUT ME*. Nottingham: NES Arnold.

Useful contacts and resources

Afasic, 50-52 Great Sutton Street, London EC1V 0DJ
Tel: 020 7490 9410   Fax: 020 7251 2834   Email: info@afasic.org.uk
Web site: www.afasic.org.uk

Department for Children, Schools and Families (DCFS), Sanctuary
Buildings, Great Smith Street, London SW1P 3BT
Tel: 0870 000 2288   Fax: 01928 794248   Email: info@dcfs.gsi.gov.uk
Web site: www.dcfs.gov.uk

The National Association for Special Educational Needs (nasen),
4/5 Amber Business Village, Amber Close, Tamworth B77 4RP
Tel: 01827 311500   Fax: 01827 313005   Email: welcome@nasen.org.uk
Web site: www.nasen.org.uk

National Children's Bureau (NCB), 8 Wakley Street, London EC1V 1NG
Tel: 020 7843 6000   Fax: 020 7278 9512
Web site: www.ncb.org.uk

Portage Early Education Programme Checklist (1987), NFER-Nelson,
Darville House, 2 Oxford Road East, Windsor SL4 1DF.

Pre-school Learning Alliance, 69 Kings Cross Road, London WC1X 9LL
Tel: 020 7833 0991   Fax: 020 7837 4942
Web site: www.pre-school.org.uk

Qualifications and Curriculum Authority (QCA), 83 Piccadilly, London
W1J 8QA
Tel: 020 7509 5555   Fax: 020 7509 6666
Web site: www.qca.org.uk

QEd Publications, 39 Weeping Cross, Stafford ST17 0DG
Tel: 01785 620364   Fax: 01785 607797   Email: orders@qed.uk.com
Web site: www.qed.uk.com